100 WAYS FOR PEOPLE TO GET HEALED

A BIBLICAL PERSPECTIVE

VOLUME 1

ALPHONSO CRAWFORD

Copyright © 2016 by Alphonso Crawford

All rights reserved. No part of this book may be reproduced or transmitted in any form or by any means without written permission of the author.

ISBN 978-0-935379-00-6

Library of Congress Control Number: 215902814

Published by New Life Educational Services
P.O. Box 96
Oak Lawn, Illinois 60454

Printed in the U.S.A.

DISCLAIMER

I am not a doctor. This book is intended for educational purposes. The main source is the Bible, the word of God. The author and publisher assume no responsibility for any risks you take regarding this information. You are responsible for your health. Check with your doctor, health care practitioner, or exercise your constitutional right.

TABLE OF CONTENTS

INTRODUCTION 6

1. ACKNOWLEDGEMENT OF GOD 8
2. ABIDE IN CHRIST 10
3. ACCEPTANCE OF SELF 12
4. ACCEPTANCE OF OTHERS 14
5. ADOPTION 16
6. ADVANCED INTERPERSONAL COMMUNICATION 18
7. AEROBIC EXERCISE 20
8. AFFIRMATIONS 22
9. AGREEMENT 24
10. AGRICULTURE 27
11. ALFALFA 30
12. ALKALINE/ACID/PH BALANCE 32
13. ALOE VERA JUICE AND OINTMENT 34
14. ALTRUISM 36
15. ANGER RESOLUTION 39
16. AAT OR ANIMAL ASSISSTED THERAPY 41
17. ANOINTING WITH OIL 44
18. APOLOGY 46

19. APPEAL TO GOD 48
20. APPLE A DAY 49
21. APRON 51
22. AROMATHERAPY 53
23. ART THERAPY 55
24. ASSERTIVENESS 57
25. ATTITUDE OF GRATITUDE 59
ABOUT THE AUTHOR 68
CONCLUSION 69

INTRODUCTION

I give honor and glory to God who is the strength of my life. God has healed me of four terminal conditions. God is the source of our healing.

Exodus 15:26: for I am the Lord that healeth thee. What was my misery has turned, now my mission and message is one of hope for those that are suffering in dire circumstances. The greatest issue today is healthcare. There is a word from the Lord, Psalm 107:20, He sent His word and healed them. Numbers 23:19, "God is not a man that He should lie; neither the son of man that He should repent: hath He said, and shall He not do it? Or hath He spoken, and shall He not make it good." God has magnified His word above His name, Psalm 138:2. I believe in the infallible, inerrant, authoritative word of God. This book was written for the sole purpose of informing you that you can enrich and extend your life with choices.

There are countless ways for people to get healed. The most effective strategies include the whole person. We are all on a quest for healing, whether it be physical, spiritual, or emotional. You can discover optimal health and wellness through establishing more balance and eliminating stressors that lead to disease or discomfort.

This book is based on the assumption that unconditional self- love and community support are two of the most powerful components when it comes to getting healed. Individually, each one of us are responsible for our own health or wellbeing. This doesn't mean that we can control whether or not we experience disease, but it does mean that we are empowered with the ability to take steps towards healing and improving our experience of life.

This is one basic principle of getting healed, but there are several others. For starters, everyone has innate healing powers. Your body is hardwired for survival. You are a whole person and not just a set of symptoms and diseases. This means that healing can come from places beyond surgery or medication.

Healing must address every facet of a person's wholeness. Thus self-treatment should involve the source of an ailment and not just the symptoms on the surface. Often the source of a physical ailment can be traced to emotional blocks or traumas.

The ways of healing aren't just physical. They involve everything you do and think. Healing is found through movement, empowerment, and spiritual exploration. When you take responsibility for your own healing, you begin a journey that might include a combination of self-acceptance, aerobic exercise, art therapy, anger resolution, aromatherapy or improving your communication or assertiveness skills. These and other integrative or alternative ways of healing will be explored in the following pages.

1. ACKNOWLEDGEMENT OF GOD

"Trust in the Lord with all thine heart; and lean not unto thine own understanding. In all thy ways acknowledge Him, and He shall direct thy paths. Be not wise in thine own eyes: fear the Lord, and depart from evil. It shall be health to thy navel and marrow to thy bones." (Proverbs 3:5-8)

Acknowledgement of God is the first way of healing in the foundational cluster of healings. In fact everything hinges upon this reality and spiritual exercise. We're reminded in the word of God from Genesis to Revelation to always remember the Lord; for it is He that gives us power to receive specified benefits from covenantal blessings. God is so considerate of His creation from the one with details, to the many, receiving collectively, showers of blessings to meet all needs.

All our needs are met in compliance with God's will. Our responsibility is one of faith and obedience. Looking to God for fulfillment of our expectations is what is expected out of us. Utter dependence upon Jehovah-Jireh will reveal Jehovah-Rapha without a doubt as our healer. As our choices through obedience in tandem with the word of God enhance our quality of life with the infusion of God's life that flows freely through our anatomy and physiology all the time.

It is incumbent upon us to remember God:

"Bless the Lord, O my soul, and forget not all His benefits: Who forgiveth all thine iniquities; who healeth all thy diseases;

(Psalm 103:2-3)

How can we forget after such wonderful acts of benevolence that are extended so graciously to us on a continuous basis. God should be first on our daily agenda in the schedule of life. That is one of the ways that we receive, maintain, and keep our healings. Healings are appropriate because there are many parts of the body that have to be attended to periodically. The intricate and complex systems of the internal environment as well as what has been noted as the trichotomy—spirit—soul—body—which requires wholeness, healings.

God in His infinite wisdom has an abundance of healing resources internally and externally beyond our scope of imagination. These ways of healing are for prevention, reversal, and recovery from life threatening infirmities. Healings in various forms are always welcomed and appreciated in extreme circumstances. Reflecting God's awesome power...His love, grace, mercy,---extended to all regardless of any irreverence on our part. His tender mercies are over all His works, love compels Him and multiplied grace is what He gives out in abundance. It is impossible to deplete the inexhaustible resources of God's storehouse.

2. ABIDE IN CHRIST

"Abide in me, and I in you. As the branch cannot bear fruit of itself, except it abide in the vine; no more can ye, except ye abide in me. I am the vine, ye are the branches: He that abideth in me, and I in him, the same bringeth forth much fruit: for without me ye can do nothing. If a man abide not in me, he is cast forth as a branch, and is withered; and men gather them, and cast them into the fire, and they are burned. If ye abide in me, and my words abide in you, ye shall ask what ye will, and it shall be done unto you." (John 15:4-7)

Tremendous benefits accrue to us when we rest in God through Jesus Christ by faith. All we have to do is ask for whatever our needs are. If we ask it will be granted to us.

There are many definitions for abide.

- Dwell
- Reside
- Live in
- Hang in there

...and many more. Dwelling in that relationship, anchors, stabilizes, fortifies, and increases your faith as you approach your heavenly Father for your many requests, foremost is your healing. With the utmost confidence, knowing that everything is going to be allright.

"He that dwelleth in the secret place of the most High shall abide under the shadow of the Almighty." (Psalm 91:1)

"He shall call upon me, and I will answer him: I will be with him in trouble; I will deliver him and honor him. With long life will I satisfy him, and show him my salvation.

(Psalm 91:15-16)

"And whatsoever ye shall ask in my name, that will I do, that the Father might be glorified in the Son. If ye shall ask anything in my name, I will do it."

(John 14:13-14)

"And in that day ye shall ask me nothing. Verily, verily I say unto you. Whatever ye shall ask the Father in my name: ask, and ye shall receive, that your joy may be full."

(John 14:24)

"The fear of the wicked, it shall come upon him: but the desire of the righteous shall be granted." (Proverbs 10:24)

3. ACCEPTANCE OF SELF

"I will praise thee; for I am fearfully and wonderfully made:

marvelous are thy works; and that my soul knoweth right well." (Psalm 139:14)

Self-acceptance is a remarkable way to get healed. To be effective, acceptance of self must be unconditional. This isn't always simple, but it is well worth the commitment. The wonderful benefits will appear instantly, filling your soul with goodness. Finding a state in which you are happy with yourself is vital to your health and wellness.

When you fail to accept yourself, this establishes an undertone of stress and negativity. It is difficult for the body to heal when it is stressed. The result can be measured in the form of increased cortisol levels. Studies show that this negative stress can also decrease your body's ability to repair damaged cells because DHEA levels drop.

Emotionally, lack of self- acceptance can interfere with your ability to love, build relationships, or enjoy life. Self-hate or judgment puts a damper on everything, preventing you from feeling free or happy. This long term distress is damaging. It can exacerbate many physical conditions such as arthritis, chronic pain, or weight management problems.

The good news is that you have everything to gain when you stop being hard on yourself. In addition to being able to take a big sigh of relief, acceptance and forgiveness are remarkable healers of the body and mind. This leads to deep relaxation and genuine joy.

Accept yourself, not just your positive attributes, but also your flaws. Accept that your body may not be flawless, but it is the one that you have and is capable of incredible things. Everyone has skills and qualities that are worth appreciating. Focus on those and forgive yourself of your shortcomings. Make peace with yourself. Be patient with yourself. God is not through with you. There are limitless opportunities for internal and external self improvement.

When you do this, you become more apt to take good care of yourself and make choices that improve your life experiences. Choose acceptance of self because it feels good and it provides a powerful way of healing.

4. ACCEPTANCE OF OTHERS

"A new commandment I give unto you, that ye love one another; as I have loved you, that ye love one another." (John 13:34)

Judging or trying to change others is an age old recipe for frustration and internal suffering. It is natural to want to change people, especially , those we care about, into the people we hoped or dreamed they would be. But it isn't possible. In the end, the only people we damage by pursuing such a mission is ourselves. The same can be said when we waste energy hating or seeking to punish those who live with different values. Instead, we must stimulate healing through the love and acceptance of others.

This doesn't always require that we agree or appreciate their words or actions, but we can make a choice to accept them for who they are, including all of their bad habits or shortcomings. It is possible to love a person while agreeing to disagree. This simple choice is so powerful. It frees you from the need to worry. When you make a vow to stop judging others, you will feel freer and lighter, as though a huge weight has been lifted. When you accept others you will be filled with peace that removes frustration, disappointment, and resentments from our hearts and minds.

We must stop spending so much energy trying to change the way others think or feel. These are things we have absolutely no control of.

Their truths belong to them and their perspective isn't filtered through the same past. We must move beyond our own labels or judgments in order to see and accept others as they are. Everyone has a path and a purpose that we may not yet understand. We can love and accept those who are different or disagree, and it all starts with a single choice. From a broader perspective, when we are able to accept others, we start to locate a deeper sense of self-acceptance as well.

5. ADOPTION

Adoption is a beautiful thing. Many families take in children as their own—some reasons include not being able to have children of their own, having big hearts and helping children to overcome previous living conditions, etc..

For many people unable to have children of their own, adoption is one of many ways. It is an answer to their hopes and dreams of having a child or children they can call their own.

Families that already have both parents and their own children can also choose to adopt a child. They are financially well off and wish to provide for another child who is looking for a family

Parents and their children alike, sometimes have the compassion on seeing those children that are in need. What better way to provide a home for them where they are truly wanted, helping someone who is less fortunate. The families are committed to welcoming a child locally, nationally, and internationally into their loving stable environment.

Adoption for anyone is a selfless and wonderful act full of compassion and love which brings healing both to those considering adoption and the adopted child/children.

Adopting a child and sharing the love they feel is an overwhelming, joyous and life changing experience.

However, adopting an abandoned child that deserves a second chance will be one of the most rewarding experiences you will ever have.

"Having predestinated us unto the adoption of children by Jesus Christ to Himself, according to the good pleasure of His will." (Ephesians 1:5)

6. ADVANCED INTERPERSONAL COMMUNICATION

"Pleasant words are as an honeycomb, sweet to the soul, and health to the bones." (Proverbs 16:24)

Communication seems like a simple skill. Anyone can talk or listen. Yet often our meanings get twisted and misinterpreted. Thankfully, it is easy to learn advanced interpersonal communication. It works by thinking carefully before we speak and choosing positive words and phrases. Good health, especially psychological health, depends on loving ourselves through kind communication and feeling as though our feelings are heard and understood.

The words we use have the power to damage or heal. They can create wounds in the heart or materialize in our bodies in the form of stress or anxiety. When those wounds go untreated, they can build and grow until they destroy. The words you choose can break, but they can also mend. They can help you rise up to a higher level. Your words can also be used to heal others.

Miscommunication can also lead to anger and distress, which can both manifest in the form of physical ailments when left unchecked. Poor communication alienates us from others and fosters a negative, violent community.

If your words have created wounds in others, it is important that you take the time and energy to mend those injuries. The same is true of any wound you have created in your own body or mind. Old wounds can grow, damaging your health and breaking important relationships.

Think of words as tiny, invisible seeds. If they are planted with the intention of healing, they will grow into good health, strength, and love. You cannot take your words back once they have been thought or spoken, but you can overpower them with positivity. The best thing about wounds created by poorly chosen words is that they are always capable of healing. Choose your words carefully. Use advanced communication skills to love, support, and encourage healing.

7. AEROBIC EXERCISE

Aerobic exercise is great at building muscles and strengthening bones. It can also help you lose weight and feel great, but the results don't stop there. Movement can actually bring healing physically, emotionally, and spiritually. Aerobic exercise has a unique ability to influence the biochemical trends happening inside you, boosting your immunity, stimulating healing, and even curing serious diseases.

New groundbreaking studies reveal that aerobic exercise is the very best medicine you can find regardless of whether you are fighting cancer, heart disease, or a simple cold. No medication or supplement comes close in terms of helping you heal faster and more effectively. Exercise even makes wounds heal more quickly.

All you need to do is to start moving. Walking, jogging, or dancing are three of the most enjoyable forms of aerobic activity. Make these types of activities part of your ordinary routine to unlock incredible benefits:

- Exercise will reduce your risk of heart disease, reduce cholesterol levels, and speed the healing of preexisting arterial damage.

- It fights osteoporosis by stimulating the growth and repair of muscles and bones.

- Movement stimulates the growth of new brain cells, preventing and even reversing age-related dementia, alzheimers's disease or cognitive decline.

- It reduces inflammatiom, which is the primary cause of arthritis, chronic pain and some cancers.

- It boosts your immunity, making you less likely to get sick and helping you recover more quickly when it can't be avoided.

- Exercise heals your mind by providing a way to release unresolved emotions while also providing clarity, boosting your mood, and combatting depression.

Aerobic exercise is an all-encompassing healer that affects just about every system within your body, improving your mind, body, and spirit. It may be the most effective way to stimulate healing and establish holistic wellness.

8. AFFIRMATIONS

Dictionary description:

Something that is affirmed; a statement or proposition that is declared to be true.

Thoughts that are repeated regularly and systematically sink into the subconscious mind and become habitual. Affirmations as these are called, are used by many children and adults to create lasting changes in their lives. Finding the right affirmations to use is much more effective if it is in your own words since the subconscious will react better to your own thoughts than to the thoughts of someone else. It is easy to understand that you would not trust anyone more than you trust yourself.

Write down on paper your thoughts, desires, and feelings that you may wish to improve upon.

How To Use Affirmations

When wording your affirmation, you need to use words and phrases for your affirmations in a positive manner rather than a negative manner. As an example, if you wanted to quit smoking, you would not want an affirmation such as "cigarette smoking makes me sick" because you will in turn cause yourself to get sick. It is better to phrase affirmations like "I am a nonsmoker" or "I am healthy and dislike the smell and taste of cigarette smoke" thereby instructing your subconscious to see a different you. When your subconscious sees yourself different, you will become different. Whatever the subconscious mind believes, the conscious mind becomes.

It is important to choose your words wisely. You do not want to use phrases like "I want" because no change will take place since your subconscious is already there. In other words, affirmations worded with "I want" simply are a statement of what "you want," this only affirms that you will always want whichever it is that your affirmations are presenting. You must see yourself as a different you by visualizing what you would like to accomplish. Use words like "I am" or "I have." this allows your subconscious to visualize and believe you are already what you wish to become instead of what you want to become.

Positive affirmations can enhance any area of your life, from improving health, skills, success, relationships, and more to conquering bad habits like unhealthy eating habits, aggressive tempers and attitudes, biting nails, bed wetting, drug addictions, or lack of attention and motivation. There are many resources available to help those who find creating affirmations to be difficult. Read the Bible and find affirmations for particular situations you confront in life, especially for healing.

9. AGREEMENT

Sickness and diseases are some undesirable circumstances that happen to people, even to us Christians. In the scriptures, great figures like Elisha, Hezekiah, and even the Apostle Paul had ailments. Nevertheless, God already has all that covered by His acts of mercy and grace. Christians who experience illness are supposed to pray to God, demanding for their healing. You ought to do so, having some sense of entitlement because the Father has all that covered by His provisions in the covenant, which was enacted when Jesus finished His work on the cross. In Mark 7:26-27, Jesus described healing as the children's bread. Also, the prophet Isaiah prophesied about this privilege (Isaiah 53:4-5).

1 Peter 2:24 confirms by saying "who His own self bare our sins in His own body on the tree, that we being dead to sins, should live unto righteousness: by whose stripes ye were healed." Apostle Peter highlighted it. Notice he indicated this healing as being in the past being concluded and sealed by Jesus 'deeds' on the cross. Therefore any child of God who doesn't ask for healing cheats himself or herself.

The Christian has to come to an agreement within him and to believe God and His word expressly. This threefold harmony between a person, God and His word is called "faith" (Mark 11:22-24,

Hebrews 4:1). It would interest you to know that faith is that force in the human spirit contending with all adverse circumstances, and places a demand on God and His resources. Faith usually acts on the platform of God's word's and promises. "But without faith it is impossible to please Him: for He that cometh to God must believe that He is, and that He is a rewarder of them that diligently seek Him."

Hebrews 11:6. It has been established that man has to agree with himself, with God, and His word. There is yet another angle to this that we will explore.

In Matthew 18:18-20, the Bible declares; "Verily I say unto you. Whatsoever ye shall bind on earth shall be bound in heaven: and whatsoever ye shall loose on earth shall be loosed in heaven. Again I say unto you, that if two of you shall agree on earth as touching anything that they shall ask, it shall be done for them of my Father which is in heaven. For where two or three are gathered together in my name, there am I in the midst of them. From this scripture we can see God's formidable promises for our healing. The first is God's power of attorney given to man to operate on earth (Psalm 115:16). We are to represent God in doing His will on the planet by doing His word. One of such is our healing and total health (III John verse 2). Therefore, when we stand in prayers to God concerning our health, He confirms it in heaven by His divine seal of the name of Jesus (Philippians 2:9).

The next basis for our healing is that of agreement between two believers. This means that God goes into action when there are at least two of His children, united in spirit and purpose, and making a healing request (or any other) to Him. This power of agreement is further elaborated for us to comprehend its limitless possibilities when He used the word "anything" in Matthew 18:19. It is therefore, crystal clear that God opens His "checkbook" and tears out a blank check slip, with our name on it whenever we unite in prayer. The last platform for our total recovery is in Matthew 18:20. He reassures us of His divine presence whenever we gather unto Him. Notice He didn't say "ten people," nor a hundred, neither did He mention a large congregation, but just "two or three." That is so simple a condition to meet to provoke heavenly emergency in our favor. The things of the spirit can be so simple, and unbelievably too simple at times that they are often doubted or overlooked.

Hello, people, sickness and diseases have no legal claim over your body. Your healing is yours for the taking when you carry out these appropriate steps at enacting God's providence over your health. Do not wallow any longer in sickness, take bold steps and enjoy God's promises.

10. AGRICULTURE

"And God said, Let the earth bring forth grass, the herb yielding seed, and the fruit tree yielding fruit after his kind, whose seed is in itself, upon the earth: and it was so. And the earth brought forth grass, and herb yielding seed after his kind: and God saw that it was good." (Genesis 1:11-12)

Soundness of health is the craving of everyone, even though many aren't doing enough to that effect. Not enough caution is applied at avoiding issues that harm the body, also less than sufficient measures are deployed to comply with even the health rules and recommendations. Though the feeling of discomfort, pain, bodily limitations and even death are enough reasons for anyone to desire healing. There is a line of divide between healing and good health. The former is a rejuvenating process from some physical ailment to wholeness. Good health is a situation whereby a person is in a state of physiological equilibrium, the whole body functioning properly in harmony to create the absence of injuries, impairment and ailments . With all this being established, we are going to take a glimpse into a factor that plays a significant role in providing healing and sustains an ideal health. In what ways does agriculture affect our health.

The Nutrients Derived From Food

The food we eat constitutes a vital aspect of our physical development and its general wellbeing.

Beyond the sweetness to our taste buds and the soothing feeling of satisfaction that comes from a full belly, there is more that food helps us to achieve. There are natural deposits in edible plants and animals (which they acquire and build up while growing until they are ready for human consumption) that our bodies desperately need to survive. These essentials are called nutrients because they nourish the body. Like fuel and oil to an engine, these nutrients from food sustain our body metabolism, help maintain our health, and keep us alive. In fact, quality diets alone can prevent bad health. When taken along with medication, nutritious foods can speedily help treat a sick person. The agriculture of plants and animals, therefore, nourishes our bodies and enhances our health.

Drugs Are Produced From Plants And Animals

There is still another means of which agriculture is a blessing to our health. Have you ever wondered what the world would be like without medical science and drugs? Probably just a handful of people would be alive and they would have dilapidated bodies. Most drugs are processed from plants of various kinds. One earlier form of this was the invention of quinine which was an effective cure for malaria. All parts of some particular shrubs, grasses, and trees are useful in pharmacology. Their roots, stems, bark, leaves, flowers, and leaves could have pharmaceutical value. Many pharmaceutical companies have farms where these essential plants are cultivated in large scale.

Also some other forms of drugs have known to be derived from animals. Even though some of these animals are classified as being wild and not reared, they are still protected and nurtured by conservation laws, which is similar to agriculture in some aspects. For instance, anti-venoms are usually extracted from poisonous snakes. Extracts from animals such as tigers, oils from snakes and fishes, honey from bees, tusks from animals have also been known to be used to achieve this aim.

A Greener And Healthier Earth

Agriculture in this context should be viewed from a wider perspective, beyond nurturing plants and animals for food and medicine. The cultivation of trees, shrubs and grasses for an environmental purpose is also inclusive. The green world that surrounds us produce quality air for us to breathe, because plants inhale carbon dioxide (what we breathe out) and exhale our oxygen (what we take in). This on its own,

creates a very healthy atmosphere for our survival. These trees and plants help to tame the disastrous effects of dangerous gases produced by pollution of all sorts. Tree planting campaigns have become more popular on a global scale as it is one great way to protect the environment and enhance our health.

Agriculture is a mandatory prerequisite for the health of humanity. These are just three ways in which plants and animals aid our existence on earth.

11. ALFALFA

Alfalfa is a plant of ancient origin, but it has now been widely used by Americans and Europeans. If there were to be anything like an unusual plant, then it would be Alfalfa, because it is so close to being miraculous. The special powers exhibited by it have been extremely beneficial to man nutritionally and health-wise. Vitamins A, B, D, E, K, magnesium, calcium, folic acid, biotin, iron, potassium, and even protein are all present in Alfalfa in rich deposits.

Alfalfa has been known to have been used as herbal medicine centuries ago, to cure various health challenges. It was initially used to feed animals in ancient times, by then its value hadn't been discovered. The rich nutrients in this plant have been believed to be as a result of its very long roots, reaching down about 18 meters into the earth. Advocates claim that it is able to absorb vast nutrients because of its deep roots. Others debunk this line of thought, feeling the plant is so because of nature's benevolence, citing instances of other plants with long roots that have little or none of such values to man. What role does Alfalfa play in our healing and health?

- The numerous vitamins and minerals found in the Alfalfa plant can be used for patients who are still sick and for those on their path to recovery. Since they would find it difficult to eat, it would act as an appetite booster, as well as a food supplement.

- The Alfalfa plant can be administered to individuals who have been malnourished for one reason or the other, since their bodies lack the necessary nutrients to function properly.

- It has inherent powers to detoxify the body and blood of harmful matters, flushing out toxins and dangerous fluids from the body.

- It helps to reduce the harmful effect of cholesterol in the body. The proteins, vitamins and minerals in them to increase the body's metabolism which sheds off excess blood fat or cholesterol.

- Alfalfa extends its healing powers to people suffering from wounds, bones and joint complications, mouth odor, headaches and even migraine.

Modes Of Administration

- Some pharmaceutical companies have developed the plant in capsule form to be taken as multivitamins and food supplements.

- Alfalfa, fresh or dried, can be taken with soups, salads, sandwiches, regular meals, as a tea or blend with certain vegetable juices.

- Use in moderation according to directions.

12. ALKALINE/ACID/PH BALANCE

PH Balance is critical to both your physical and mental health as well as your well- being. High acidity can become a dangerous condition that weakens all major body systems. It makes your internal environment conducive to disease. A ph balanced environment, on the otherhand , allows proper metabolic functioning and gives your body resistance to disease. Your body is constantly working, 24-7 to maintain a delicate balance between acidity and alkalinity. Everything you ingest-but also the environment-the air you breathe and the emotions you experience—all contribute to your

ph (which stands for "potential Hydrogen").

What Is A Healthy, Balanced PH?

The ph scale runs from 0 to 14. Our blood must maintain a slightly alkaline 7.365 ph. A healthy body maintains alkaline reserves that are used to meet emergency demands. Low ph can mean symptoms and disease.

Cellular nourishment is vital to health!

Each and every cell in your body must breathe fully and the oxygenation of each cell depends upon having an optimum ph balance. To get the idea of how important oxygen is to your life, just stop breathing for a minute. As previously stated, when ph is off and our bodies become more acidic, our cells are getting less oxygen. Cancer thrives under an acidic tissue ph/oxygen deficient (anaerobic) environment. Is it any wonder today that cancer rates are up?

13. ALOE VERA JUICE AND OINTMENT

"As the valleys are they spread forth, as gardens by the river's side, as the trees of lign aloes, which the Lord hath planted, and as cedar trees beside the waters." (Numbers 24:6)

"All thy garments smell of myrrh, and aloes, and cassia, out of the ivory palaces, whereby they have made thee glad."

(Psalm 45:8)

"I have perfumed my bed with myrrh, aloes, and cinnamon."

(Proverbs 7:17)

Aloe Vera is a popular modern remedy that dates back to ancient Egypt, where it was rumored to be the secret of immortality. Today it is mostly used to treat less lofty ailments, like sunburn or indigestion. The plant itself is actually a variety of cactus. When the plant is broken, you will discover a clear gel with a fresh gentle scent. This gel makes a convenient ointment to encourage healing. The plant can also be processed to produce juice that can be consumed to treat several disorders related to digestion and elimination.

Aloe Vera is soothing to the skin. It spreads healing and can often prevent scarring. It's efficacy has been proved through countless scientific studies. In addition to helping people get healed, Aloe Vera juice and ointment have several additional benefits.

It is nontoxic, all natural, and gentle on the body. It can be applied directly to the skin and contains its own preservative qualities. In addition to healing, it is nourishing for the skin and hair, which means it is handy for treating acne, canker sores, and eczema, hand even scalp issues like dandruff.

The more we learn about aloe, the more uses we uncover. It can be used to treat wounds and burns of all types, though its cooling sensation is especially welcome on sunburns. It has antibacterial properties that combat skin infection or herpes, and astringent properties that make it official for treating cysts. Its nutritive qualities make it perfect for diabetes. When ingested, Aloe Vera can even lower cholesterol levels. Plus, its anti-aging and moisturizing effects are great for your skin. With all of these healing benefits, it's no wonder the Egyptians considered Aloe Vera to be the key to immortality. It is certainly a valuable tool for healing.

14. ALTRUISM

"Knowing that whatsoever good thing any man doeth, the same shall he receive of the Lord, whether he be bond or free."

(Ephesians 6:8)

Altruism simply means attitude of love of neighbor or absence of selfishness. A selfless person is one who thinks of others before thinking of his/herself. Altruism is one of the bases of various religious doctrines like Christianity, for example. In the case of Christianity, altruism is revealed through the love of neighbor, one of the commandments left by Jesus

(John 13:34). Nevertheless, altruism is not an exclusive attitude of a person who follows a religion and can be demonstrated by anyone as a matter of morality.

A selfless individual self seeking, and not helping others in order to obtain some benefit in return. The act of giving comes with a lot of benefits to the giver. Even a small act of kindness can have emotional benefits. The point of engaging in helping behaviors is to transform your own heartbreak into a story of kindness.

Improvement In Mental Health

Altruism, positive physiological changes in the brain associated with happiness. The peak periods are often followed by longer calm and can eventually lead to greater well being. Helping others to improve

social support, leads to a lifestyle more physically active, and takes our mind off of our own problems. It allows us to engage in meaningful activity and improves our self-esteem and competence.

It Brings A Sense Of Integration And Reduces Isolation

Being part of a social network leads to a sense of integration. Interpersonal activities such as volunteering at a shelter can help reduce loneliness and isolation.

Help Perspective

Helping those that are in situations of need, especially those who have been less fortunate than us, can provide a more realistic perspective and become aware of how blessed we are; allowing us to stop thinking about what we lack and help us to take a more positive view on what might be causing us stress.

Improved Confidence, Control, Happiness, And Optimism

An act of generosity can also encourage others to repeat the good action. It can also contribute to the promotion of good works in the community; making it more positive.

The more you do for others, the more you do for yourself. The evidence shows that the benefits of helping others can last long after providing a 'bank' of pleasant memories that can be retraced in the future.

Physical Benefits

Helping others contributes to good health. Positive emotions reduce stress and strengthen our immune system and thus protect us against disease. Partaking in acts of altruism can make a person suffering with sadness, depression or any negative feelings that affect mood feel better. It reduces our negative feelings and emotions. Negative feelings like anger, aggression or hostility have a negative impact on our mind and body. Participating in all kinds of acts of generosity can help reduce these feelings and stabilize our overall health. The act of giving and helping others could lengthen our lives. Studies show that those that support others live longer than those who do not.

15. ANGER RESOLUTION

"Be not hasty in thy spirit to be angry: for anger rests in the bosom of fools." (Ecclesiastes 7:9)

One of the most powerful emotions is anger. When it arises appropriately and is effectively resolved, anger can be a positive, self-preserving emotion. However, poor anger management can destroy you from the inside out. Nurturing and fostering anger produces negative medical conditions in your body. When left unchecked, it can destroy your health and your relationships.

Feelings of anger stimulate your fight or flight response. This is a good thing if you are in immediate, physical danger, but it can cause harm when you visit the response too often. When the response is triggered, your adrenal glands release stress hormones including cortisol and adrenaline. At the same time, your body prioritizes your blood volume, sending it away from your stomach, possibly interrupting digestion, and flooding your muscles. In addition to feeling enraged, your heart rate speeds up, your temperature rises, your blood pressure increases, and your breathing quickens.

This surge of hormones coupled with the metabolic adjustments can lead to headaches, digestion disorders, stomach pain, sleeplessness, anxiety, depression, high blood pressure, heart disease, cardiac arrest, skin rashes, and even stroke.

Burying your anger can be dangerous. When it isn't resolved, it grows beneath the surface where it will ultimately surface as these physical maladies. The key to resolving anger is being aware of yourself and your emotions.

You will need to identify the source of your anger, recognize it, find validation, and then seek a healthy resolution, perhaps by changing your perspective or talking it out calmly. You might consider releasing it through physical activity, relaxation techniques, prayer, or professional counseling sessions. It is vital to establish habits that solve internal conflicts as they arise so that they do not build into uncontrollable rage.

"Make no friendship with an angry man; and with a furious man thou shalt not go. Lest thou learn his ways, and get a snare to thy soul." (Proverbs 22:24-25)

Anger resolution will help iniate healings in your spirit, soul, and body.

16. AAT OR ANIMAL ASSISSTED THERAPY

Animal Assisted Therapy is an area that has received increased attention in therapeutic recreation. This therapy is a form of treatment that pairs animals with specific traits, and patients with specific needs. AAT can be a valuable aid of treatment for those people who are socially, emotionally or cognitively challenged. In recent years, medical experts have been relying on Animal Assisted Therapy as a valuable aid in reaching out to the elderly, the infirmed, and to ill or abused children.

An animal does not have the power to heal, but through its affection and unconditional love, it can promote relaxation, stability, and help address critical situations with greater serenity. Positive emotions from the comfort animals have been found, in this sense, to be an excellent antidote against diseases. Comfort animals improve physical, emotional, and cognitive function in many patients as well as reducing loneliness. Sometimes just one treatment can and does work in alleviating many symptoms.

AAT provides a social context for people suffering from emotional and mental ailments to share time with family members in a comfortable, non-confrontational atmosphere. Petting and stroking an animal allows the patient a degree of physical intimacy sometimes no longer possible between patient and caregiver. The therapy can have a positive effect on the patient's physical health, as well as on his or her emotional health creating a sense of purpose. For example, when a person is suffering from arthritis pain in their hands, having a good pet like a dog or cat to brush the hands out from time to time or on a daily basis can be a great source of treatment. It is nice to be able to move the hands in a motion that will make the person feel good and also allow them the opportunity to make the dog feel better too. This is a good way to get started with a great recovery processs for any person that wants to get their feeling back and do the things

that they once did. When a person is faced with the fear that they will lose mobility, they can turn to the animal assisted therapy program and it can help them cope with their pain.

For the lonely elderly patients, AAT is particularly valuable in reducing isolation—holding a warm puppy or playful kitten provides the unconditional love they need so much. For patients having dementia, ATT can prolong viable home care options by reducing confusion, improving clarity and assisting with memory function. Particularly in seniors who were lifelong pet lovers, it is a window into the past allowing elderly patients to recall long forgotten animal companions. Anecdotal evidence reports that patients with advanced Alzheimers's saw a marked reduction in anxiety and agitation when receiving regular AAT.

The ideal therapy pet must be gentle and placid, never aggressive. While a variety of animals are used in AAT, dogs are particularly well suited for therapy sessions with elderly patients. ATT also promotes physical movement , emotional well being, cognitive awareness and social improvement for people with disabilities. In a health care facility, people can come out of their rooms to socialize with the animals and with each other.

Finally, although ATT has been shown to be effective for many people, it is important to remember that not everyone enjoys the presence of animals. Like any other type of therapeutic intervention, AAT should take the patient's likes and dislikes into account. Overall, participating in any type of animal assisted therapy program can be a rewarding experience for everyone involved. To find an AAT near you, look for a program with clear, therapeutic goals for its participants and infection control guidelines that insure the safety of the patient. Also, be sure to get approval from your doctor before starting any visits.

17. ANOINTING WITH OIL

"And they cast out many devils, and anointed with oil many that were sick, and healed them." (Mark 6:13)

In biblical times, it was common to anoint the sick with oil as a modality of healing. It is a tradition that continues in many communities today. Jesus would often lay hands on the sick before He healed them. He would often instruct His disciples to heal the sick by laying their hands and anointing them with oil. Let's explore the ways in which anointing the sick with oil is an effective means for stimulating many types of healing.

In centuries past, the oil extracted from crushed olives was used as a medicine. Though olive oil is used to treat a few mild ailments today, there are certainly more potent remedies available for most physical ailments. Yet that doesn't mean that they are necessarily more effective. There are many components to healing and while some are physical, the physical and psychological cannot be denied.

The blessed oil used in healing is representative of the Holy Spirit. It champions belief and intensifies the genuine power of prayer. Together this bolsters the healing process. In the New Testament, we learn of anointing with oil as a means for praying for the sick. So much of belief is internal and invisible, that small rituals, such as anointing with oil, provide a powerful medicine that is both seen and felt.

Throughout the Bible, the elders are encouraged to do this for the sick and the weak in order to call upon God's healing power. It is an act of God's love and encouragement. In this way the oil and the associated human contact are not merely medicine, but a conduit through which the Holy Spirit arrives, bolstering the faith and strength of the recipient. In essence, the anointing oil strengthens and symbolizes faith, which is itself healing in countless ways.

18. APOLOGY

Most of the time, we wrong other people, mistakenly or deliberately. The issue is not that whether we hurt somebody's feelings but how we deal with the fact we have offended others. In that regard we need to apologize. An apology is one of the most effective means to reconcile conflict between individuals, families, groups and even nations. Without an apology, the offended will harbor anger and resentment, seeking some kind of justice or revenge. A sincere apology makes resolution possible. It can bring comfort and solace to the offended, relief to the wrongdoer and healing to their relationship.

So many people may see apology as a sign of weakness, but it is not. It is an act of humility, honesty, and courage. A sincere apology will bring about forgiveness and reunion. This is what the power of apology will do. It will do away with restrictions that hold people back from having satisfying relationships with one another.

When you refuse to apologize, you form a barrier in the relationship with those you wronged. That barrier will linger and the fabric of relationship will depreciate. Great relationships are products of a willingness to make an apology, to forgive and forget, and to reconcile. Without those components, relationships will remain cold, shallow, and distant.

Some wounds can only be healed by a sincere apology and nothing more. However, an apology may not be effective except it is accompanied by some form of restitution, compensation, reimbursement, and gift.

For the specific wrong done or injury inflicted on a person, admit that you are wrong. Do not make excuses by stating reasons you couldn't get it right.

Show Sincere Remorse

Try and let the offended know that you are genuinely sorry for what you did. Human beings are a bundle of emotions. When you wrong someone, you hurt the person's emotions. So when you apologize, let the offended see your sincerity and remorsefulness.

Make It Timely

Nothing beats doing the right thing at the right time. Always know when the time is right to apologize. If your apology comes to quickly, chances are it will be less effective. The offended is possibly still angry. If it comes to late, it will not be effective, instead it will trigger the person's resentment the more. But then all things being equal, your apology should come sooner than later.

19. APPEAL TO GOD

Hezekiah was given a death sentence. What recourse do you have when you are given a death sentence? An appeal to the courts of our Lord is in order. God reversed Hezekiah's dilemma because of his sincere petition. (Hezekiah 38:1-9)

Healing is one thing that many people seek in the world. God is the source of healing. He is the source of solving all problems and can heal you of anything, any disease that you are afflicted with.

Isaiah the 53rd chapter gives a dramatic and detailed account of what Christ suffered to purchase our salvation. Included in that premium package was healing for the nations. This is our blessed assurance. We can count on Him and His Father to hasten to perform His word.

So whenever our mortal body is weak and our spirit seems to wonder, we should still remain calm and have faith in God. We should key into His grace with directions from the scriptures, believe in His truth and submit ourselves to His mercy; this way we will be healed of whatever troubles us and this kind of healing is everlasting.

20. APPLE A DAY

We all know how the saying goes, "an apple a day keeps the doctor away." Not only do apples taste good, but they are good for you too. They have many health and healing benefits that can keep you out of the doctor's office and keep your body healthy and looking good. Here are the top reasons why apples should be in your diet.

Reduces The Risk Of Heart Disease

Apples contain high levels of flavonoids which are important when it comes to fighting heart disease. Every time you consume an apple, these flavonoids which are called catechins help to fight off this disease and diseases like it.

Boost Your Immune System

Vitamin C is a very important vitamin that helps to keep your immune system working properly and keeps you from catching that cold you have been dreading. Apples contain more than 1500 mg of vitamin C. Almost half of the vitamin C content is just beneath the skin. Eating an apple a day may keep you away from the doctor by boosting your immune system.

Lowers Cholesterol

Another great aspect of apples is they can lower the bad cholesterol in your blood. Apples contain soluble fiber called pectin, this helps to lower cholesterol in your body. Apples also contain flavonoids, anthocyanin, and phenols which all help in the oxidation of low density lipoprotein, which is bad cholesterol.

Nature's Candy

Although most people have only tasted about two types of apples (Granny Smith and Red Delicious), there are hundreds of varieties of apples and they all have their own unique taste. Apples are crunchy, sweet, tart, and juicy; everything that makes an apple nature's true candy!

Improves The Health Of Your Lungs

Apples contain nutrients in them that help to prevent asthma or even lung cancer. Research has shown that those who eat more apples, at least five per week were less likely to have a disease related to their lungs and will cough or wheeze less often. If you eat at least five apples a week you will surely find yourself breathing better and having a healthier respiratory system.

Plenty Of Ways To Eat Them

Apples can be used in almost any way you can think of. Apple pie, apple juice, apple chips, apple crisp, hair products, applesauce are just some of the ways you can use apples. There are plenty of other ways you can use apples.

21. APRON

"And God wrought special miracles by the hands of Paul: So that from his body were brought unto the sick hankerchiefs or aprons, and the diseases departed from them, and the evil spirits went out of them." (Acts 19:11-12)

Just as God's healing power was delivered to the sick in the time of Acts, today the transfer of divine energy continues to be shared through aprons or hankerchiefs. Once blessed and prayed over, these become prayer cloths that deliver healing. In most churches an elder will pray over a hankerchief or apron as they did in Acts. The healing operates through faith, as the wearer accepts God's healing power through the anointed cloth.

Some healing modalities escape science, yet their validity is proven through centuries of firsthand accounts. The same can be said of apron/hankerchief healing. Numerous stories have been told of positive results, namely healing of the discovery of peace. The recipient wholeheartedly believes that they will be healed through the touch of God, making the cloth powerful and effective as it promotes healing and/or deliverance.

Apron/hankerchief healing operates through God's love and the miracle of His sacrifice. When materials are prayed over and blessed in this manner, people are cleansed of disease or evil and simultaneously charged with the beauty of the Holy Spirit.

This is why an anointed cloth must be handled with respect and care in order to preserve its ability to stimulate incredible healing.

The recipient of the cloth should wear it close to the source of their ailment. This is often done through pinning the cloth beneath their clothes. It should not be removed until its work is complete. It is essential to note that the cloth cannot work on its own. It must be accepted with faith and prayer. The person must trust in God's intention to deliver the right type of healing at exactly the right time.

22. AROMATHERAPY

"All thy garments smell of myrrh, and aloes and cassia, out of thy ivory palaces, whereby they have made thee glad."

(Psalm 45:8)

The scents of concentrated plant extracts have long been popular in cosmetics and beauty supplies. Now research confirms that they also have healing benefits as well. Essential oils in particular have the ability to safeguard your health, eliminate discomforts, and even cure certain diseases. In fact, most natural scents carry powerful healing abilities. Some reduce stress and ease pain while others will boost your mood or calm an upset stomach.

Aromatherapy works when a scent is inhaled. This activates a place in your brain called the hypothalamus, a control center which manages your hormones, energy levels, and many other body functions. Studies show that different scents trigger different effects. For example, some tell your central nervous system to relax while others wake it up and tell you to remain alert. Following are a few examples of healing scents:

Sage: In addition to improving your memory and focus, smelling sage also has the healing benefit of reducing your blood pressure and respiration rate.

Orange: The scent of orange provides a pleasant way to instantly boost your mood; it also curbs anxiety. People who sniff orange report feeling calmer and less stressed. It works by stimulating a drop in the presence of stress hormones.

Lavender: This one is perhaps the most popular. Lavender can encourage relaxation. It also reduces insomnia, depression and even migraine pain.

Some scents, particularly in the essential oil form, are powerful. This means that careful handling is in order as too much can cause a negative effect. It is important to follow the directions on the bottle carefully and limit therapeutic sessions to no more than sixty minutes. Of course, if you have a chronic illness, it is important to discuss any healing regime with your doctor. When these guidelines are followed, aromatherapy can create impressive results.

23. ART THERAPY

"The light of the eyes rejoiceth the heart." (Proverbs 15:30)

The things you see can change your physiology and the way you think. You probably already know that some spaces make you irritable while others make you feel calm or energized. Color has a huge impact on your physical body. In fact, art has the ability to iniate healing or cause infirmities. This is what makes art therapy so effective.

Through art therapy, people can create and immerse themselves in images that nurture and heal. In general, the colors used in art therapy are divided into two categories: cool or warm. Warm colors include hues like sunny yellow or fiery reds, while cool colors include purples, blues and greens. Depending on their tone, cool colors can be sad or calming. Warm colors are often described as being comforting, angry, or hostile. Research has demonstrated that violent or scary images, particularly those featuring the color red, can cause your heart o race and your adrenaline to spike.

The colors and images that you encounter most have the most significant effects. If you need to reduce your blood pressure or slow your respiration, for example if you are battling heart disease, then you should engage calming colors to create a serene environment. Meanwhile, those who are tired and lethargic can benefit from bright bursts of warm colors framed in a positive manner to prevent irritation. These tones can also improve your appetite.

Studies show that art therapy is great for people who suffer from physical illness. Research involving cancer patients showed that art therapy can reduce symptoms of pain, depression and anxiety. Participants are invited to resolve issues by expressing themselves artistically, eliminating stress, recognizing problems, and building confidence. Art therapy doesn't require creative skills, only a desire to find healing.

24. ASSERTIVENESS

"But speaking the truth in love, may grow up into Him in all things, which is the head, even Christ." (Ephesians 4:15)

Being assertive isn't just a useful communication skill. Assertiveness means you have the ability to express your thoughts and feelings. This gives you the ability to stand up for yourself and demand the tools you need to heal. It is the key to real healing. Far too many people hold back, suppressing their true emotions because they are worried that others might judge them or respond unfavorably. There is also sometimes a fear of hurting someone else's feelings

Instead, we hurt ourselves. We push our feelings deep inside until they begin to manifest as stress, anxiety, or even depression. It can show up as physical symptoms too, such as insomnia, panic attacks, stomach disturbances, or chronic pain. When this is the cause of our suffering, the only way to stimulate healing is by learning to be more assertive. It is important to be able to express yourself and stand up for your needs or beliefs without harming others.

Being assertive doesn't only improve your ability to manage and release stress. It also will help foster greater confidence and earn more respect from others. One of the most valuable assertiveness skills is the ability to say no. Permit yourself to say no to anything you do not want to do or have done to you. This unlocks the ability to control your life.

While some people are inherently assertive, anyone can learn to become that way. The first thing is to respect youself and your own wishes. The next is to continuously remind yourself that your emotions are just as valid as others. Another way is to stand tall and speak respectfully. This encourages those around you to stop, listen, and to take you seriously. You don't need to yell or act erratically in order to be heard.

25. ATTITUDE OF GRATITUDE

"So we thy people and sheep of thy pasture will give Thee thanks for ever: we will show forth Thy praise to all generations." (Psalm 79:13)

Having an attitude of gratitude is good for your health. Everyone is familiar with the expression,

"True beauty comes from within." Well it turns out that this statement is actually quite true. Recent studies has shown that creating an "attitude of gratitude" in your thoughts not only makes you feel good, but can even contribute to healing your body of chronic diseases!

When you feel good, the body responds by boosting its natural ability to heal itself. Think about it for a moment when you are having negative emotions like fear, resentment, anger and jealousy, your thoughts are also negative. These negative thoughts then actually produce chemicals in the brain and body that cause negative physical feelings in the body, such as anxiety, fatigue and even pain.

You could be wondering: Why should I be thankful? Being thankful calms your spirit, emotions, mind and body, increases your energy; restores your health and expands your understanding, knowledge and creativity. It makes you positive, confident, pleasant, friendly, cheerful, carefree, good hearted. Being thankful takes away sorrow, regret, anguish, heartache, stress, worry, depression and fear.

Of course, we face challenges and setbacks in life, but when we are thankful in whatever adversity we encounter, we will come out of it being a stronger person by learning from it. Living in gratitude attracts every valuable thing God has to offer, and everything our heart desires, and they will be ours when we receive everything with thankfulness.

BOOKS BY ALPHONSO CRAWFORD:

- LIFE'S WAY UNTIL: POEMS ON FAITH/HOPE/SALVATION
- TWO HEARTS: LOVE POEMS
- LOVE LETTERS
- CROSSROADS: POEMS ON RACE/POLITICS/LIFE
- WISDOM: 25 FACTS ABOUT WISDOM
- TRIUMPHANT: 25 WAYS TO EXCEL IN LIFE
- 100 WAYS FOR PEOPLE TO GET HEALED: VOLUMES 1-4

FORTHCOMING BOOKS BY ALPHONSO CRAWFORD:

- 100 SYMBOLS OF HEALTH AND HEALING: VOLUMES 1-4
- ADVANCED HEALING MANUAL
- THE THREE GREATEST CHALLENGES OF LIFE: 25 TESTS
- DOMINATE: 25 DOMINION PRINCIPLES
- POWER: 25 FACTS ABOUT POWER
- WOMEN HAVE POWER: 25 POWERS WOMEN POSSESS

- WHY GOD MADE BLACK PEOPLE BLACK
- LEADERS: 25 FACTS ABOUT LEADERS
- LEADERSHIP: 25 PITFALLS/POWERTOOLS
- LEADERSHIP IN AGE OF CRISIS: 25 OBSERVATIONS
- LEADERSHIP: TOUGH QUESTIONS/TOUGH ANSWERS
- GOD'S WILL: 25 WAYS TO KNOW GOD'S WILL FOR YOUR LIFE
- DREAMS: 25 FEATURES OF A DREAM
- ADVANCED INTERPERSONAL COMMUNICATION: 25 WAYS TO EXPRESS YOURSELF
- SPIRITUOTHERAPY:25 PRINCIPLES
- PERSONALITY PROFILES: A BIBLICAL PERSPECTIVE
- MEN: 25 FACTS ABOUT MEN
- HEALTH AND HEALING WORKBOOK: 25 ACTIVITIES
- HEALTH AND HEALING DEVOTIONAL BOOK
- HEALTH AND HEALING QUIZ BOOK
- THE POWER OF BIG THINKING: 25 PRINCIPLES
- HEART: 25 FACTS ABOUT THE HEART

- BLOOD: 25 FACTS ABOUT THE BLOOD
- HEALTH AND HEALING AFFIRMATION BOOK

BOOKS BY ELEANOR CRAWFORD:

- WOMEN IN MINISTRY: 25 WAYS TO IMPACT THE WORLD
- WOMEN OF DESTINY: 25 CHALLENGES WOMEN FACE
- THE WOMAN A MYSTERY: 25 FACTS ABOUT WOMEN
- WOMEN IN HISTORY: 25 WOMEN WHO CHANGED HISTORY

FORTHCOMING BOOKS BY ELEANOR CRAWFORD:

- WOMEN'S RESOURCES: 25 ASSETS
- WOMEN OF WISDOM: 25 INSIGHTS
- WOMEN'S MANUAL: 25 LIFE LESSONS
- WOMEN'S WORKBOOK: 25 ACTIVITIES
- WOMEN'S DEVOTIONAL BOOK
- WOMEN'S AFFIRMATION BOOK

- WOMEN'S SERMONS: 25 SERMONS
- WOMEN AND MEN: 25 CONTRASTS

BOOKS BY BYRON CRAWFORD:

- SUCCESS IN LIFE: 25 STEPS TO THE TOP
- LAWS OF SUCCESS: 25 LAWS OF SUCCESS
- SYNONYMS OF SUCCESS: 25 SYNONYMS
- SUCCESS UNLIMITED: 25 KEYS THAT UNLOCK DOORS

FORTHCOMING BOOKS BY BYRON CRAWFORD:

- SELL YOUR WAY TO SUCCESS: 25 WAYS TO SUCCEED IN LIFE
- SECRETS OF SUCCESS: 25 SECRETS OF SUCCESS
- SUCCESS MANUAL: 25 LIFE LESSONS
- SUCCESS WORKBOOK: 25 ACTIVITIES
- SUCCESS STRATEGIC PLANNING: 25 TACTICS
- SUCCESS SERMONS: 25 SERMONS
- SUCCESS QUIZ BOOK

- SUCCESS DEVOTIONAL BOOK
- SUCCESS AFFIRMATION BOOK

SIGN UP AND BE NOTIFIED FOR SEMINARS/WORKSHOPS/CONFERENCES

NAME_____

ADDRESS_____

CITY_____

STATE_____

ZIP
CODE_____

PHONE
NO._____

EMAIL_____

SEND TO:

NEW LIFE EDUCATIONAL SERVICES

P.O. BOX 96

OAK LAWN, ILLINOIS 60454

SEMINARS/WORKSHOPS/CONFERENCES

- ANNUAL WOMEN'S LUNCHEON
- ANNUAL MEN'S LUNCHEON
- HEALTH AND HEALING
- DREAMS AND VISIONS
- PERSONAL POWER
- GIFTS AND TALENTS
- PROBLEM SOLVING
- RELATIONSHIPS
- INTERPRETING CURRENT TRENDS
- ADVANCED INTERPERSONAL COMMUNICATION

- ADVANCED STRATEGIC PLANNING
- MANAGING SELF
- MANAGING CONFLICT
- MANAGING STRESS
- LAWS OF POWER
- NEGOTIATION SKILLS
- BIG THINKING POWER
- STRATEGIES FOR SUCCESS

- HOW TO SELL YOURSELF
- GLOBAL STEWARDSHIP
- HOW TO COUNSEL
- SELF MOTIVATION
- PEOPLE MOTIVATION
- APOSTOLIC/PROPHETIC CONFERENCE
- TEAM BUILDING
- VISION
- TIME MANAGEMENT
- SETTING GOALS
- CHANGE AGENTS
- WEALTH IN YOU
- FEEDBACK
- NEEDS OF MEN/NEEDS OF WOMEN
- SELF DECEPTION: HOW WE LIE TO OURSELVES EVERYDAY
- LIFE SKILLS
- HOW TO START A CHRISTIAN SCHOOL
- HOW TO HOME SCHOOL

ABOUT THE AUTHOR

Dr. Alphonso Crawford is an Apostle of health and healing. Dr. Crawford is the president of New Life Educational Services. He pastors Cathedral Of Prayer with his wife. Dr. Crawford received his background in biblical studies from Moody Bible Institute. He holds the B.A. from DePaul University, the Master Of Divinity from McCormick Theological Seminary, the Doctor of Ministry from Chicago Theological Seminary, respectively at the University of Chicago.

CONCLUSION

Health is simply a condition of being sound in the body, mind and spirit. It describes the general condition of the body, illness on the other hand is an unhealthy condition of the body, or mind. It is a state when the body or mind is weakened, disordered or unsound. God's best and desire for us is sound health (III John 2).

Many fall sick in their bodies and in their minds for various reasons. For example, many are sick bodily because they lack wisdom on how to take good care of their bodies. They just keep on using their bodies until it reaches it's breaking point. Some on the other hand allow the cares of this life to really weigh them down. They start by getting worried and then their condition graduates to depression. These are just a few examples of the many reasons believers and unbelievers alike fall ill. However, if we act on the word, we can live sickness free lives. If you don't rest your body properly, you will be afflicted and conflicted.

Is there a balm in Gilead? Thank God there is. Adequate provision has been made available for us in the event we fall sick. That provision is called healing. God has provided many resources for our healing. And our lives can be enhanced and enriched through the choices we make.

www.ingramcontent.com/pod-product-compliance
Lightning Source LLC
Chambersburg PA
CBHW060427050426
42449CB00009B/2165